The Nature Kid's Guide to
SQUIRRELS

DAVID ANDERSON

LP Media Inc. Publishing

For information address LP Media Inc. Publishing,
30012 Variolite St NW, Princeton MN 55371
www.lpmedia.org

Publication Data

Squirrels
The Nature Kid's Guide to Squirrels — First edition.

Summary: "Learn all about Squirrels, the Nature Kid Way"
— Provided by publisher.

ISBN: 979-8-89818-174-1

[1. Squirrels – Non-Fiction] I. Title.

Title: The Nature Kid's Guide to Squirrels

CONTENTS

TREE TIME

A squirrel's leaf nest is called a **drey**. It can be up to two feet wide!

Skitter! A gray squirrel races right up a tall oak tree.

Squirrels need places with plenty of trees. Trees give them everything they need: food, branches to run along, and safe spots to sleep. A squirrel without trees would be like a fish without water.

Most squirrels live in forests where tall trees grow close together. Thick woods give them places to hide from hawks, owls, and other **predators**.

But squirrels also do well in parks, neighborhoods, and towns. As long as there are trees that drop nuts and seeds, squirrels can make a home. They build their leafy nests high in the branches, or tucked into cozy tree hollows when it gets cold.

SQUIRRELS WORLDWIDE

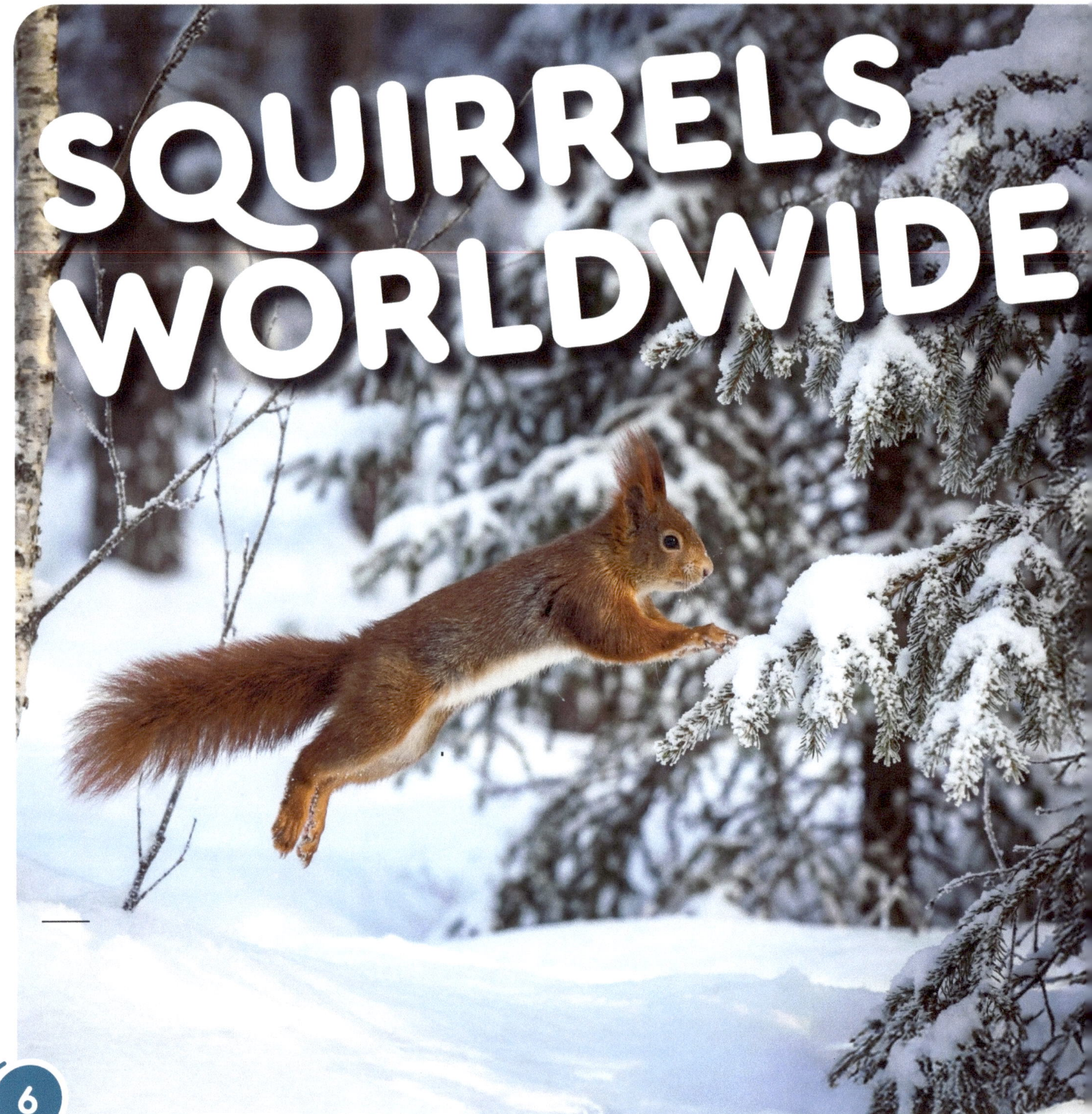

Whoosh! A red squirrel darts through a snowy forest.

Squirrels live all over the world. You can find them living on every continent except Australia and Antarctica.

Red squirrels love cold, snowy woods. They live in parts of Europe and North America. Other kinds of squirrels live in warm, sunny places.

From big parks to tall mountains, squirrels have spread far and wide. They know how to find food and homes in many kinds of spots.

There are over 200 different kinds of squirrels in the world!

SMALL STUFF

The smallest squirrel in the world is the African Pygmy Squirrel. It's only about five inches long!

Zip! A tiny flying squirrel glides between two trees.

Most squirrels are small. A gray squirrel is only about 10 inches long. It weighs about 1 pound. That light body helps it race up trees and leap from branch to branch.

Flying squirrels are even smaller, some can even fit in your hand! They are one of the tiniest squirrels around.

Fox squirrels are the biggest tree squirrels in North America. They can be as long as a house cat. But they weigh a lot less.

BUSHY BODIES

Flick! A fox squirrel waves its big, fluffy tail in the air.

Squirrels have light bodies built for climbing. Their back legs are long and strong. Sharp claws grip bark like tiny hooks.

A squirrel's tail is almost as long as its body. The tail helps with balance on thin branches. It also works like a blanket on cold nights.

Fox squirrels can have brown, gray, or red fur. Thick fur keeps them warm all winter long. Some gray squirrels can even be all black. The American red squirrel has rusty red fur and a bright white belly.

Each kind of squirrel has its own look.

SUPER SNIFFERS

Sniff, sniff! A gray squirrel smells a nut under the dirt.

Squirrels have a super sense of smell. A gray squirrel can sniff out nuts buried in the ground. Even under deep snow they can still smell them!

Squirrels have big eyes that sit on the sides of their head. This lets them see all around at once, so nothing sneaks up on them!

Sharp ears pick up soft sounds from far away. A snap of a twig means danger is close. Smell, sight, and hearing all keep squirrels safe.

Flying squirrels can make ultrasonic chirps that people can't hear!

TRICKY
TAILS

Puff! A gray squirrel fluffs its tail to look big and scary.

A squirrel's tail is its best defense. When danger comes close, the squirrel puffs up its tail. This makes it look much bigger.

Sometimes a squirrel flicks its tail very fast. This can trick a hungry hunter. The hunter stares at the tail and misses the body.

If grabbed by the tail, a squirrel may lose some fur. But it can still get away! The tail fur grows back over time.

A squirrel's tail works like an umbrella. In the rain, a squirrel holds its tail over its head to keep dry!

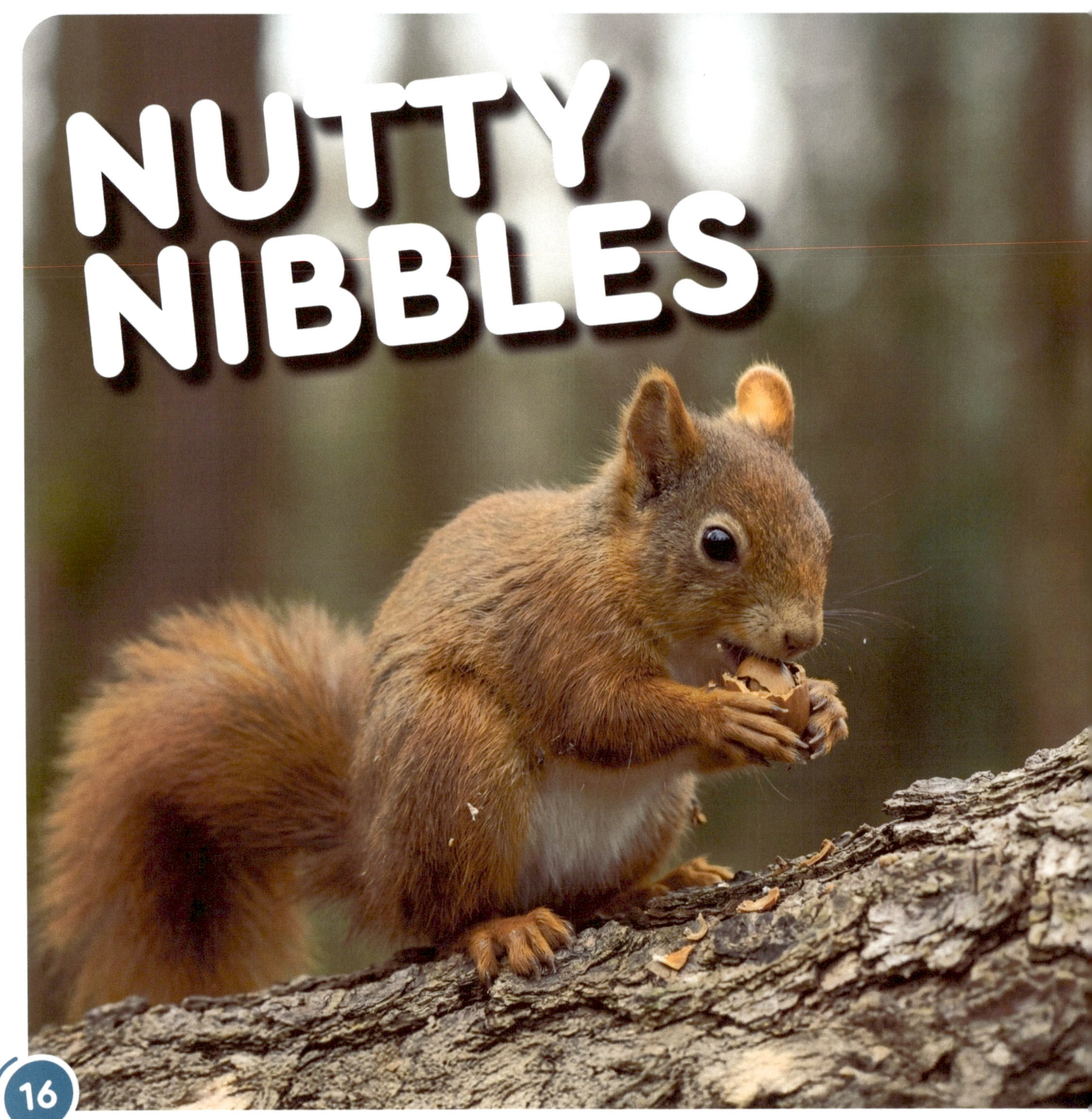

16

Crunch! A squirrel bites through the hard shell of an acorn.

Squirrels love to eat nuts. Acorns, walnuts, and pecans top the list. But nuts are not all they eat!

Red squirrels are pine cone experts. They rip apart cones to reach the tiny seeds inside. Other squirrels munch on berries, mushrooms, and even bugs.

In the fall, squirrels bury nuts in the ground for later. They dig them up when food is hard to find. This is called **caching**.

Squirrels sometimes forget where they bury many of their nuts, and new trees grow there!

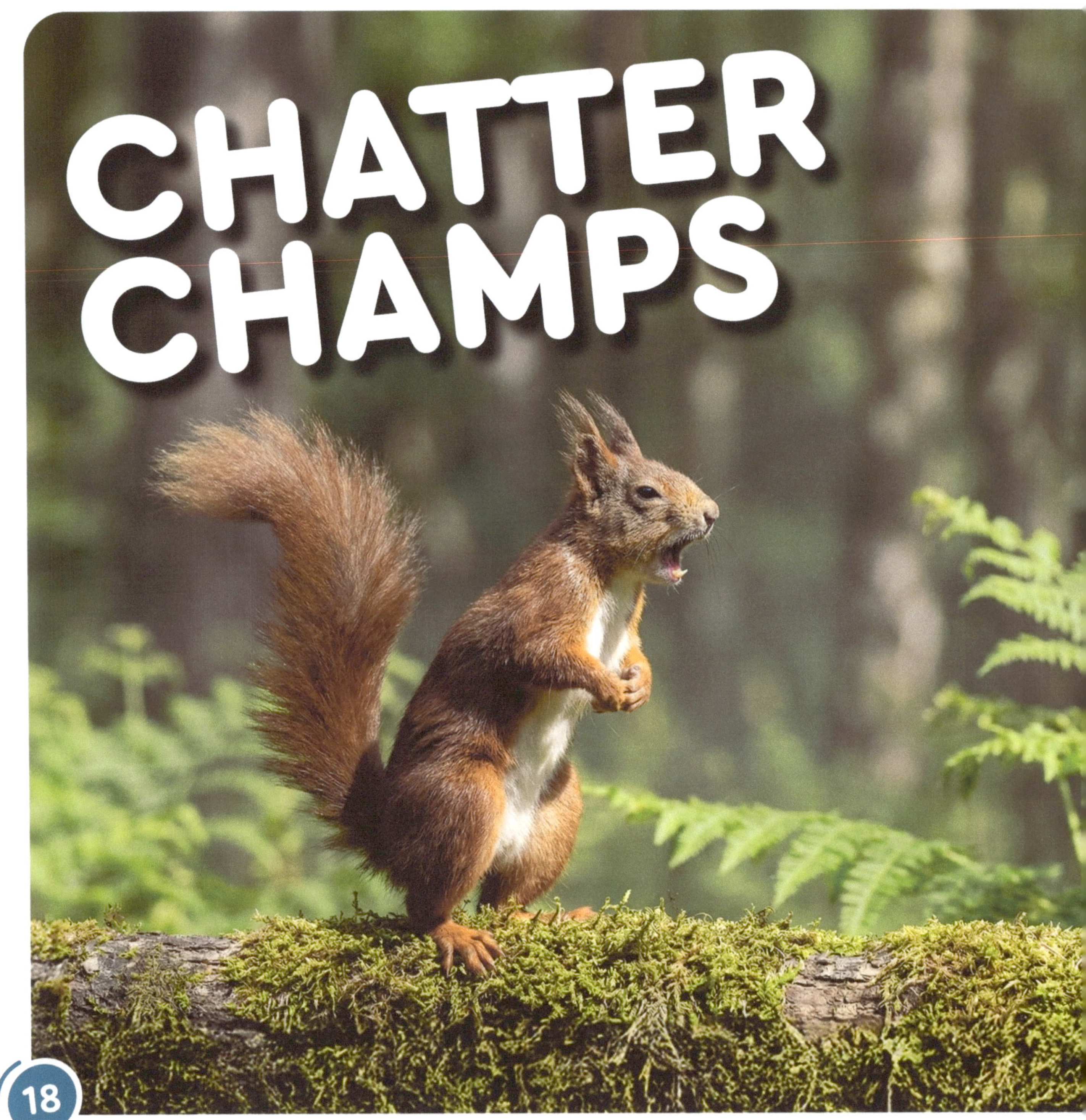

CHATTER CHAMPS

Kuk-kuk-kuk! A red squirrel screams from a high branch.

Squirrels are noisy! Red squirrels make a sharp sound called a kuk. They use it to tell others to stay away from their trees.

Squirrels also chirp, bark, and squeal. Each sound has a meaning. A high chirp may warn of a hawk. A low bark may mean a cat is near.

Stomping feet is another way squirrels talk. They slap the ground to send a warning. Other squirrels feel the shaking and run for cover.

Mother squirrels can tell their own babies apart just by sound!

WATCH OUT

Screech! A hawk dives from the sky. The squirrel sprints away!

Squirrels have many predators. Hawks, owls, and eagles hunt them from the sky. On the ground, foxes and coyotes give chase.

Snakes can climb trees to reach squirrel nests. They may eat baby squirrels inside. House cats also hunt squirrels in yards and parks.

Life is full of danger for a squirrel. They must watch and listen all day long. Quick thinking helps them stay safe.

When one squirrel spots a predator, it lets out a loud chirping alarm call. Every squirrel nearby hears it and dashes for cover!

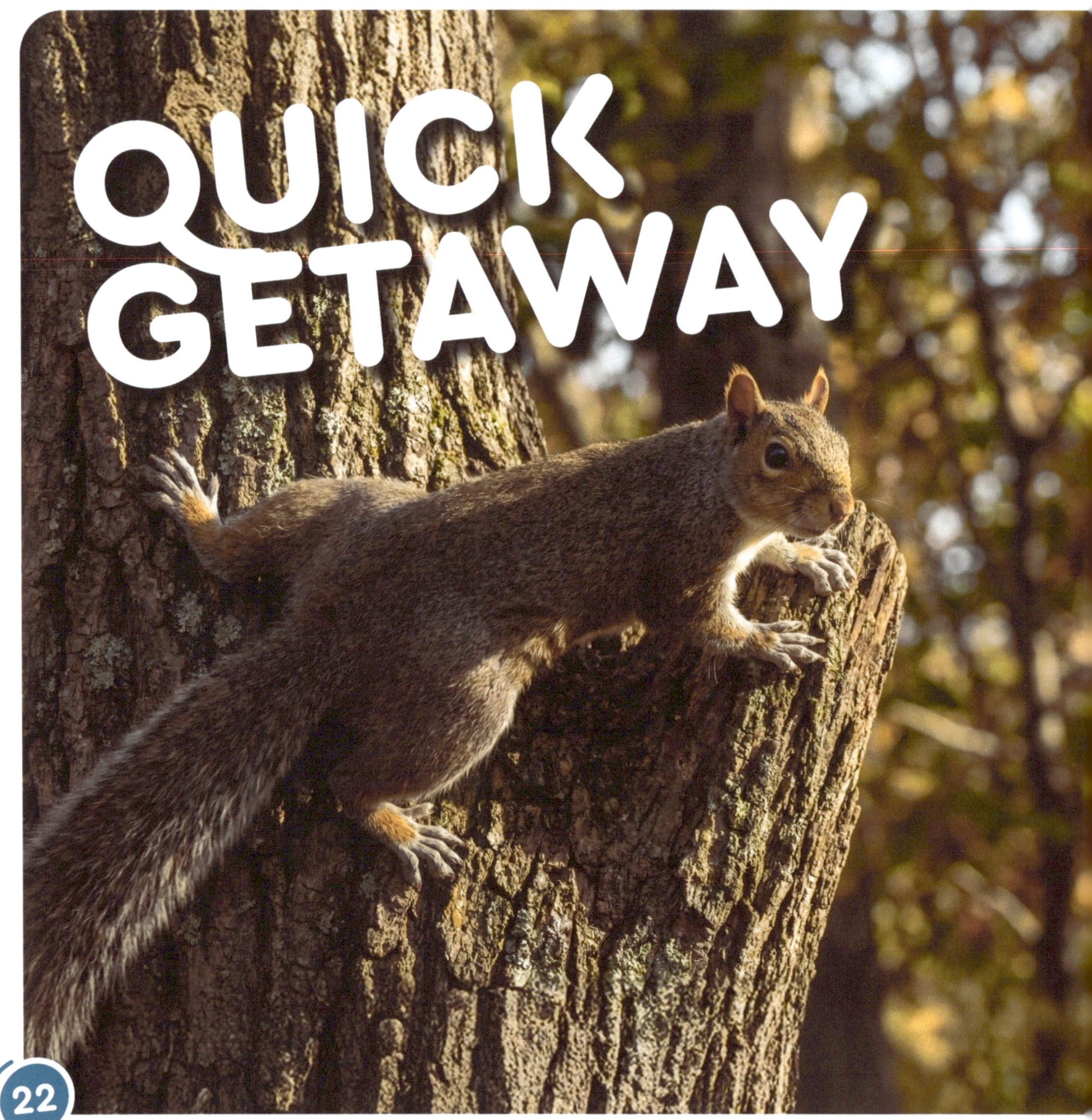

QUICK
GETAWAY

Zoom! A squirrel zips up a tree trunk in under two seconds.

When danger is near, a squirrel runs fast. It zigzags across the ground to lose a chaser. Then it races up the nearest tree.

Once in the tree, the squirrel freezes. It presses flat against the bark and stays still. Its brown fur blends right in.

If there is no tree close by, a squirrel may drop flat on the ground. It holds very still and hopes its fur hides it.

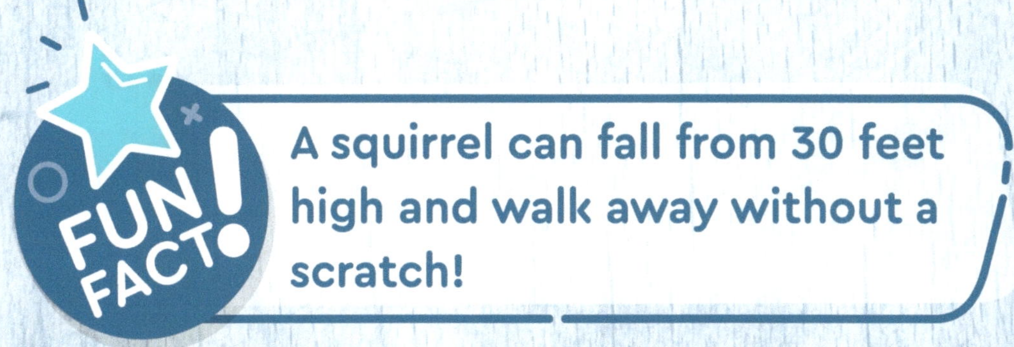

LEAP AND CLIMB

Swish! A flying squirrel sails through the dark night sky.

Squirrels are great climbers and jumpers. They can leap up to ten times their body length!

Flying squirrels do not really fly. Flaps of skin stretch from their arms to their legs. They **glide** from tree to tree like tiny kites.

On the ground, squirrels run in quick bursts. They can twist and turn in a flash. When going down a tree, they flip their back feet to grip the bark better.

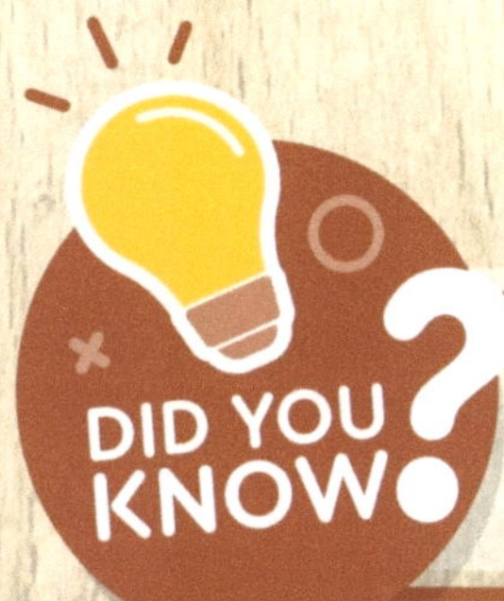

A flying squirrel can glide over 150 feet in one single leap!

BUSY DAYS

Scratch, scratch! A squirrel digs in the yard at first light.

Squirrels wake up early. Most are busy in the morning and late afternoon. They rest during the hottest part of the day.

A squirrel spends most of its day looking for food. It digs, climbs, and searches for hours. In fall, it works extra hard to store nuts.

Grooming takes time too. Squirrels lick and comb their fur to stay clean. They also stretch out on branches to soak up the sun and warm up.

In the summer squirrels will sometimes lie flat on cool pavement to cool down!

SOLO SCURRIERS

Chit! A fox squirrel chatters at a stranger near its tree.

Most squirrels live alone. They do not travel in packs. Each squirrel finds its own food and makes its own nest.

Fox squirrels guard their space. They chase away other squirrels that come too close. A loud chatter tells others to stay away!

In winter, squirrels may share a nest to stay warm. They curl up together on the coldest nights. But when spring comes, they go back to living alone.

Up to nine squirrels have been found sharing one winter nest!

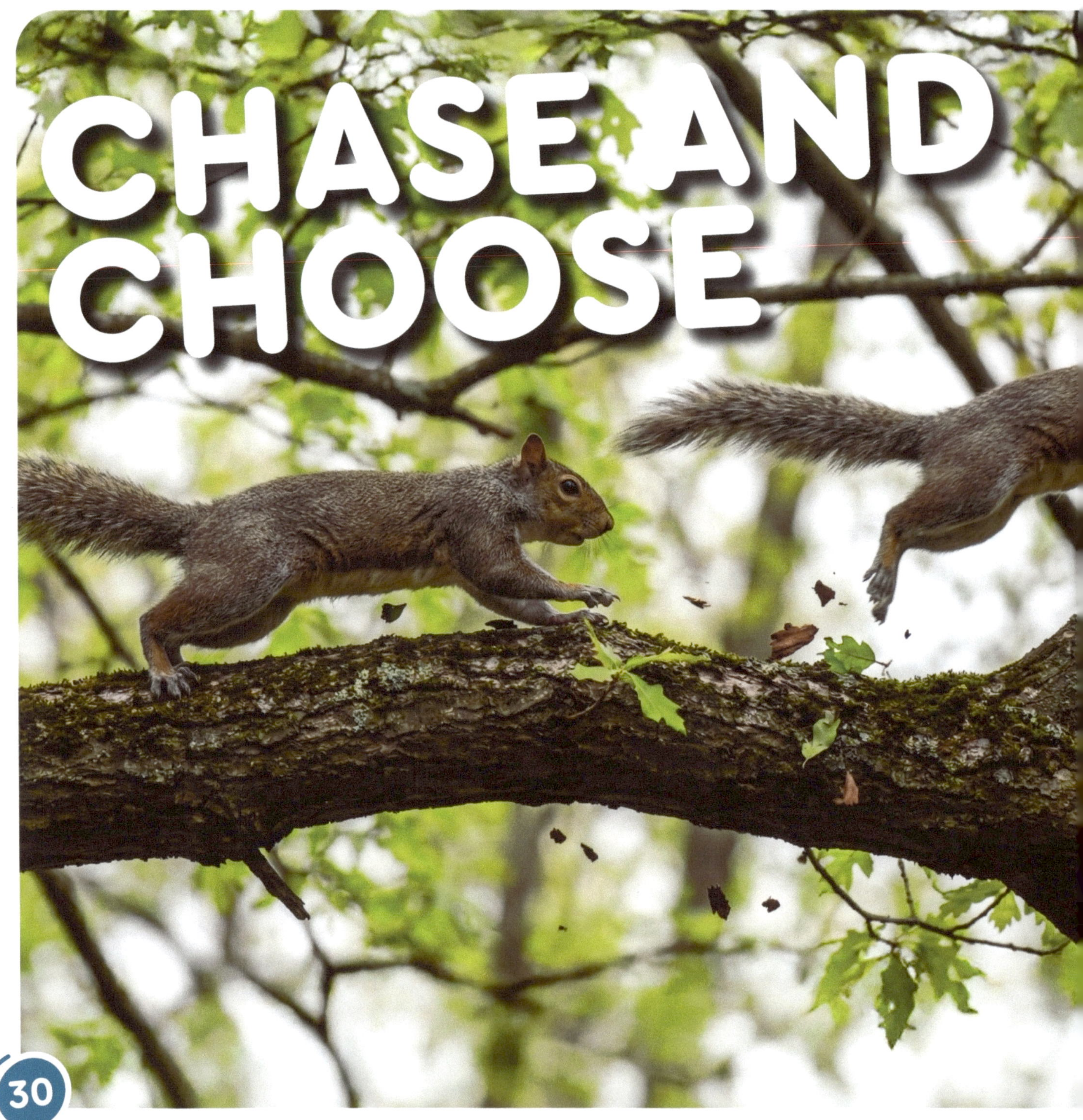

CHASE AND CHOOSE

Rustle! A male squirrel chases a female through the treetops.

When it is time to mate, male squirrels put on a show. They chase females through the trees for hours. The fastest, strongest male often wins.

Gray squirrels mate twice a year. This happens in late winter and again in summer. Males follow the scent of a female to find her.

After mating, the male leaves. The female gets ready to raise her babies on her own. She will do all the work herself.

A male squirrel may fight other males by boxing with its front paws!

TINY KITS

Squeak! A baby squirrel snuggles in a cozy tree nest.

Baby squirrels are called **kits**. They are born blind, deaf, and hairless. A newborn kit is about the size of your thumb.

Kits drink their mother's milk for the first weeks. Their eyes open after about five weeks. Soon, soft fur begins to grow all over.

Kits start to explore outside the nest at about six weeks. They cling to branches and take wobbly steps. These first trips are short but brave.

A squirrel mom can have two to five babies in a single litter!

MOM KNOWS BEST

Mother squirrels sometimes adopt lost babies from other families!

Poof! The mother squirrel carries her baby to a brand-new nest.

Mother squirrels do everything for their young. They keep the kits warm, clean, and fed. Fathers do not help at all.

If the nest is in danger, the mother acts fast. She picks up each kit in her mouth, one by one. Then she carries them to a safer spot.

Mothers teach their young to climb, jump, and find food. After about three months, the kits leave the nest for good. They are ready for life on their own.

BORN WINNERS

Brr! A black squirrel tucks into its warm tree hole for winter.

Squirrels are great at staying alive. They have survived on earth for a long time. Their skills help them handle all kinds of danger.

They have adapted to freezing mountain peaks, steamy tropical jungles, dry deserts, and busy city streets.

Their bodies adapt too. Black squirrels, which are really gray squirrels with dark fur, soak up more heat from the sun, helping them survive in colder places.

No matter what nature throws at them, squirrels find a way to handle it.

SPOT A SQUIRREL
FUN FACT!
The red giant flying squirrel lives in the forests of Southeast Asia and is one of the biggest squirrels in the world!
38

Tap-tap-tap! A squirrel runs along a fence right in front of you.

You can spot squirrels almost anywhere. Look in parks, backyards, and near big trees. Early morning is the best time to watch.

Find a quiet spot and sit down. Stay still and listen for rustling leaves. A squirrel may peek out from behind a branch.

Watch how it moves and eats. See how it leaps, climbs, and digs. Every squirrel you see is working hard to survive.

GLOSSARY

Drey

A round nest made of leaves and twigs in a tree.

Predator

An animal that hunts other animals for food.

Caching

Hiding food in a safe spot to eat later.

Kit

A baby squirrel.

Glide

To float smoothly through the air without flapping wings.